Ten Lives of the Buddha
The Silent Prince

BY

S.P. Somtow

Ten Lives of the Buddha
The Silent Prince

by S.P. Somtow
published by Diplodocus Press

The text is by S.P. Somtow, which is the literary pseudonym of Somtow Sucharitkul

Illustrations prompted, selected, edited and overseen by Somtow Sucharitkul, who is a human being, with the assistance of (but not "generated by") AI, which is not a human being

© 2025 by Somtow Sucharitkul

Dedication

The conductor from Houston, Viswa Subbaraman, talked me into writing an opera on this subject.

Eventually it grew into a cycle of ten operas, each one dealing with one of the ten lives of the Buddha, a crucial series of stories told in the Pali canon of Buddhism.

I would like to dedicate this book to Viswa in thanks for setting me off on this pathway.

The Queen of Kashi

This story happened in an ancient kingdom, a very long time ago. Perhaps a thousand years ago, or many, many more.

There was a city named Kashi, and even then, the city was ancient. The Queen of Kashi, whose name was Chandri Devi, was sad, because she knew her husband, the King, wanted to have a son.

One day, she knelt down and prayed to Indra, who ruled over the Heaven of Thirty-Three Gods.

The Heaven of Thirty-Three

Indra was the Lord of the Heaven of Thirty-Three. But he was not Lord of the entire Universe. Above this heaven were many other heavens, and in one of the highest of all there dwelt the Bodhisattva.

The Bodhisattva was a being who had already been born in the world hundreds of times, each time coming closer to finding the answer to an eternal question: "What is the cause of suffering?"

Indra asked the Bodhisattva to descend into the world and be born as a mortal being once more.

The Bodhisattva replied, "I shall go."

The Birth of Temiya

Queen Chandra Devi was delighted to learn that her prayer would soon be answered, and that she would give birth to a child.

The courtiers waited eagerly for the Queen to give birth.

On that day, a violent storm threatened the city of Kashi, and the King, who was hunting in the forest, did not return to the palace until nightfall.

Child of the Tempest

When the King arrived, the child was descending from heaven, carried by angels.

The newly born child was aware of his surroundings, because he was the incarnated spirit of the Boddhisattva.

Seeing that a storm was raging, he silenced the tempest with a single gesture.

"I bore him in a tempest," said the Queen. "I shall name him Temiya."

The King and Queen were delighted with their child, and the King swore that Temiya would lack nothing.

A Golden Chariot

When Temiya came of age, the King said, "You must put away your toys, for you have become a man now. No more toy chariots! You shall have a real chariot!"

Temiya was thrilled and proud of the gift.

"But I have another gift for you as well," the King said. "One day you will become King like me. And you must learn how it is to be a King."

The Criminal

"Look, son," the King said. "This is an evil man. He is a murderer. He has taken the lives of innocent people. As King, you will have to sit in judgment, and decide the fates of criminals."

The King of Kashi handed Temiya his sword of power, and said, "Today I give you the power of life and death. Give the command, and this evil man will perish."

Yama, the King of the Dead

Prince Temiya had a vision. He saw Yama, the King of the Dead. Yama said, "Defy your father. Everything dies anyway, and the power is in your hands."

But the Prince thought: "I am the Bodhisattva. It is wrong for me to kill. I have journeyed through hundreds of lifetimes, trying to live a pure life, so that I can understand human suffering. If I take a life, I will have taken this journey for nothing."

Maya, Goddess of Illusion

Then came Maya, the goddess of illusion.

She said to the young prince, "Obey your father and accept your destiny. I will make you rich. You will have gold, jewels, and beautiful women. All you have to do is order this worthless criminal to be killed."

But the prince thought, "We are taught to honor our parents. It is wrong to disobey my father, who is trying to teach me how to be a king."

Temiya's Dilemma

Temiya thought, "I cannot disobey my father, yet I cannot take a life. The only way that I can avoid wrongdoing is to never to respond at all."

So wrenching was Temiya's dilemma that he collapsed, fainting, on the floor of the palace.

The courtiers were afraid for his life. But when Prince Temiya awakened, it seemed that he had lost the power of speech.

Temiya Grows Older

As the prince grew in stature and beauty, he still would not speak. Instead, he would look from his window and gaze upon the suffering of his people.

And always he would wonder, "How can I end my people's suffering?"

The Mystery of Life and Death

At times Temiya would wander to the river's edge, and would watch funeral ceremonies.

Always he would ask, "Why is there suffering? Why is there sickness, old age, and death?"

He had already spent hundreds of lifetimes pondering this question.

Chandra Devi's Sorrow

The years went by and still the prince said not a word.

When he was not wandering the city, he would sit in meditation. Often he would sit motionless for days on end.

Seeing him not respond to her words, Prince Temiya's mother, the Queen, wept.

The Dancing Girls

The King had another idea. "Surely," he said, "if some beautiful women were to dance for him, he would take notice, and show his pleasure by speaking!"

The King brought the most beautiful women in the kingdom to dance before Prince Temiya.

But the prince would not be roused from his meditations.

King for a Day

The King said, "I will make Temiya king for a day. He will ride an elephant through the city and greet the cheering crowds. Surely he will come to his senses!"

Dutifully, Temiya rode through the city. Yet he did not speak.

The King is Enraged

When he realized that Temiya was still not speaking, the King of Kashi decided that he had had enough of his stubbornness. He summoned his trusty charioteer, Sunanda.

"Take my son into the forest," he said, "and don't come back until you have executed him."

Queen Chandra Devi pleaded for their son's life, but the King said, "You shall have other sons. Let us forget that this one ever came into our lives."

The Queen Weeps

Queen Chandra Devi wept, but the King's heart was hardened. He had had high hopes for his only son. He could not bear to see his hopes dashed.

He turned away as Chandra Devi watched Sunanda and the soldiers take her son towards the dark forest.

SUNANDA

Sunanda took the prince into the forest and began to dig. The prince did not protest, but sat in meditation, seeming to be indifferent to his fate.

As he dug, Sunanda realized that it would be a terrible thing to kill the young man whom he had loved and served since he was born. But he could not disobey his master, the King of Kashi.

When he had dug deeply enough to bury the prince, he heard a quiet voice call out his name.

"Sunanda," the voice said.

The Bodhisattva Speaks

"My Lord!" Sunanda exclaimed. "You can speak! Yet you have not uttered a word, even when your father condemned you to death."

"That is true, Sunanda," said Temiya. "But I cannot stand by and allow you to take a life, because you will have to atone in suffering through many afterlives. I could not let you bring so much suffering on yourself. For I am the Bodhisattva, and I have come to the world again and again, to learn to solve the mystery of suffering, and I will return again and again until I receive enlightenment."

The King Relents

No sooner had Sunanda departed than the King relented, for he loved his son. "I love Temiya more even than my kingdom," he said. "If only I could give my kingdom to have him back! But I cannot, for a king's word can never be unspoken."

Chandra Devi said, "But if you gave up your kingdom, you will no longer be king; then your command can be rescinded."

"You are right," said the King of Kashi. "Let us go to the forest now, and let us tell Sunanda that I have renounced the throne, and that Temiya shall henceforth be King."

Into the Forest

When the King announced that he would give up the throne, and henceforth live humbly in penitence and simplicity, his courtiers all decided to follow him into the forest.

When they reached the place of execution, however, what they saw amazed them.

There stood Prince Temiya, cloaked in a shimmering heavenly light.

The boy who had lost the power of speech was no longer a silent prince.

Amba

When she saw this miracle, Amba, the prince's nurse, fell to her knees.

"Do not worship me," said Temiya. "I am not a god. I am only a seeker of truth. You nurtured me and sustained me in my childhood. Do not kneel before me now."

The King and Queen of Kashi

One by one the members of the court prostrated themselves before the Bodhisattva, and to each he said, "Do not worship me, for I am a human being like you."

The Bodhisattva said, "From my home in the highest of heavens, I have heard the cries of millions of souls, human and animal, gods and demons, in world upon world. For generations upon generations I have been reborn in the world, on a quest to find a solution to the riddle of suffering.

"Only a few lives remain before I shall achieve enlightenment."

The Tavatimsa Heaven

The heavens opened, and the citizens of Kashi saw a stairway into the sky. They saw Indra, the King of the Heaven of Thirty-Three Gods, and all the gods, goddesses and angels.

The great god looked down on the world below and spoke to the citizens of Kashi.

"A King's command may not be unspoken," he said, "yet the King of Kashi sacrificed his kingship to save his son's life. The sacrifice shall not be in vain. All of you have played your part in the journey that the Bodhisattva has taken."

The King Gives Up His Crown

The King and Queen removed their crowns and laid them at the Bodhisattva's feet.

Henceforth they would be his followers. They would live a simple life in the forest.

The Bodhisattva Ascends

All watched as the Bodhisattva ascended the stairway to the heavens. He remained among the gods for a while. The he returned to the world.

He would live out this incarnation as a hermit, simply, without the luxury of a royal palace and the riches of a kingdom.

The Tavatimsa Heaven

One day, he would return once more to heaven, but he would travel beyond even the paradise of the Thirty-Three Gods.

He would ascend past heaven after heaven, until he reached the abode of absolute stillness, beyond desire.

In the highest of heavens, the Bodhisattva would wait until the next time he would descend to the world of humans.

Nine More Lives

The Bodhisattva had been reborn more than six hundred times. His soul had been reincarnated in the form of animals, dragons, and human beings.

The lesson that he learned as Temiya was the lesson of silence.

He had learned to choose silence over power. In a world that rewarded heroic achievements, victories, successes, he learned that all these things comes at the cost of suffering for others, and for oneself.

Nine more times the Bodhisattva would be reborn, and nine more lessons he would learn, before he was ready to become the Enlightened One.

The Author

S.P. Somtow is the literary pseudonym of Thailand National Artist Somtow Sucharitkul, who is most well known as an award-winning writer of novels and a composer of operas.

The Illustrator

The illustrator is a just a computer who has been manipulated by the author into producing many, many images which were then edited and reedited by the author. To call it artificial "intelligence" is, frankly, a stretch.

A Note from the Author

I am not really known for children's picture books, as most of my novels are written for decidedly more grownup readers. I also compose music, and I have written over a dozen operas. It's because of the operas that I have come to compile a series of ten books in which I retell the ten lives of the Buddha, a much-loved part of the Pali canon of texts which are the principal sources of Theravada Buddhism as practiced in Sri Lanka and Southeast Asia.

The tales are a little bit akin to parables in the New Testament. Each is a story from which one learns a moral lesson. The difference is that at the end of each narrative, the Buddha inserts himself into the story, explaining that it was a tale he himself lived through in a past life, and that the disciples listening were also role-players in the story. Over time, more than six hundred stories became associated with the *Jatakas Tales*, including folk tales that may have predated the Buddha's lifetime, or that came from other cultures like Persia. Therefore the stories are often viewed metaphorically, rather than as literal past lives of the Buddha.

The last ten lives in the series form a sequence that is highly venerated in Theravada Buddhist countries, frequently illustrated on temple walls and told to children.

In *DasJati,* my cycle of ten stage works, I use modern resources of theater, opera, and ballet to tell the stories, framing them in way that should be accessible to modern generations. This series of picture books goes along with the stage works, and the re-tellings are based on the stage adaptations of the stories rather than the original Pali language text in which some of the stories go to a hundred pages and bring in many generations and subplots.

My hope is that presenting the stories in this way will make them available not only to children but to adults who may be interested in the stories that are told in Buddhist countries which form an important communal strand in the cultures of the region.

—S.P. Somtow

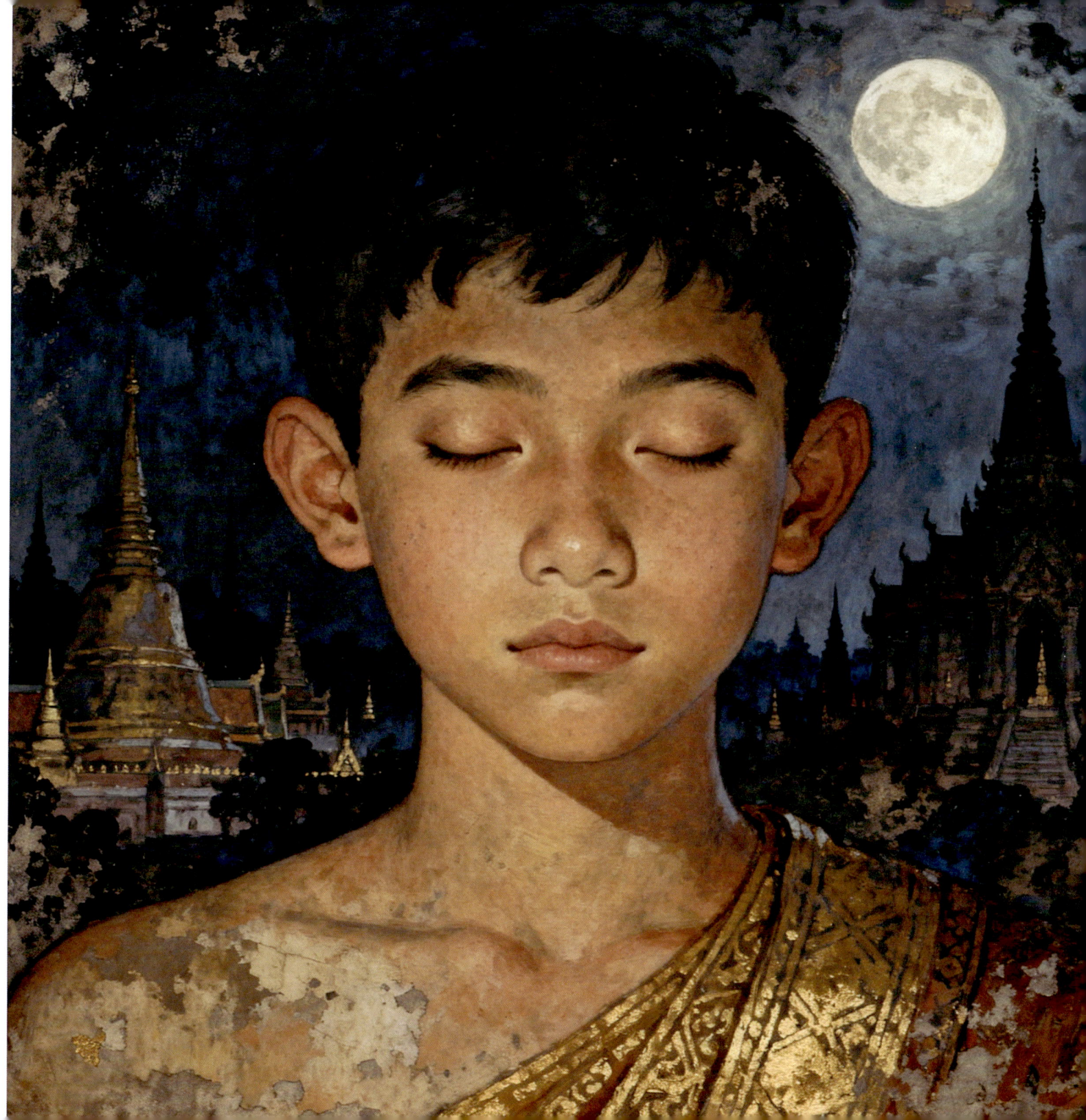

www.ingramcontent.com/pod-product-compliance
Lightning Source LLC
Chambersburg PA
CBRC090910230426
43673CB00017B/423